Propaganda

Other titles in the Teen Issues *series:*

Propaganda

Understanding the Power of Persuasion

Ray Spangenburg and Kit Moser

Enslow Publishers, Inc.

40 Industrial Road   PO Box 38
Box 398   Aldershot
Berkeley Heights, NJ 07922   Hants GU12 6BP
USA   UK

http://www.enslow.com

In memory of Mencken
the skeptical dog,
named after H. L. Mencken,
a famous critical thinker

Library of Congress Cataloging-in-Publication Data

Spangenburg, Ray, 1939–
    Propaganda : understanding the power of persuasion / Ray Spangenburg
and Kit Moser.
        p. cm. — (Teen issues)
    Includes bibliographical references and index.
    ISBN 0-7660-1664-1
    1. Propaganda—Juvenile literature. 2. Persuasion (Psychology)—Juvenile
literature. I. Moser, Diane, 1944– II. Title. III. Series.
    HM1231 .S63   2002
    303.3'75—dc21

                                                        2001008627

Printed in the United States of America

10 9 8 7 6 5 4 3 2 1

To Our Readers:
We have done our best to make sure all Internet Addresses in this book were active and
appropriate when we went to press. However, the author and the publisher have no
control over and assume no liability for the material available on those Internet sites or
on other Web sites they may link to. Any comments or suggestions can be sent by e-mail
to comments@enslow.com or to the address on the back cover.

Illustration Credits: American Cancer Society, p. 15; Eyewire, pp. 49, 52; FDR
Library, p. 27; National Archives, p. 21; Painet Inc., p. 9; Punch, 1915, p. 32;
The Reference Center for Marxist Studies, p. 37; William Whittman/Painet
Inc., p. 54.

Cover Illustration: Digital Vision.

Contents

Acknowledgments

Thank you to everyone who spent time talking with us about propaganda, persuasion, and cons and ways to think critically about what we see, read, and hear. A special thank you to CSICOP fellows Bob Steiner, Robert Sheaffer, James Randi, and Jill Tartar; Massimo Polidoro, cofounder of the Italian Committee for the Investigation of Claims of the Paranormal; Shawn Carlson, founder of the Society for Amateur Scientists; and all our friends from the Sacramento Organization for Rational Thinking.

Preface:
Get Ready to Duck!

Most people do not think of themselves as targets. Yet, at some point of the day, anyone could be the object of someone else's aim—so get ready to duck. Manufacturers and shopkeepers try to convince shoppers to buy their products. Students may try to tell their friends which candidate they should vote for in a school election. Maybe a door-to-door vendor or a friend wants us to subscribe to a magazine. Maybe they want money to help pay for a class trip or another good cause. Sometimes they are selling a lifestyle. Sometimes they are selling alcohol, cigarettes, or drugs. These people taking aim may have innocent motives, or they may be cheats. They may mean no harm, or they may not care what happens to their targets. Usually, they have their own objectives and interests in mind.

These people are all trying to persuade. They use a group of methods known as *propaganda*—a systematic effort to convince people to take a specific action or adopt a point of view. There is nothing wrong with that. However, often these methods include unfair tricks. Sometimes, even when people are working for a good cause, they mix truth and fiction. Propaganda often sways people to act without thinking. Even if the methods are not unfair, persuaders almost always use powerful ways to attract attention and make a point. Propaganda usually appeals more to emotions than to brain power. And emotions can fool us.

Propaganda has a bad reputation. Political propagandists and con artists often lie about their "facts" and purposely trick people to gain power or money. Under the influence of propaganda, victims sometimes give away money they cannot afford to give. People may vote for a corrupt leader because they believe the campaign propaganda. Worse, especially during wartime, everyday citizens may become convinced that innocent victims deserve to be put in prison or put to death.

For most people, though, the most easily recognized propaganda appears in ads—in magazines, on television, on billboards. Consider these examples:

- A clothing store Web site carries the photo of a good-looking boy. "Is this guy your type?" the big letters ask.

- "Buy the best, by any test!" a television commercial yelps.

- A short-haired teen leans against a city wall, feet crossed, hands in pockets. She wears the latest look in clothes. What is this black-and-white photograph about? Only a close look reveals a clothing designer's name on the label across her shirt pocket.

What is going on in these three situations? They are all ads, or commercials. Each one carries the same message: Buy our product. These ads are one form of propaganda. Propaganda tries to persuade or convince. People who create propaganda may have positive motives; they may have evil motives. They may be innocent; they may be dangerous. They all have one trait in common,

Advertisers and other propagandists appeal to our emotions. For example, beverage producers might use a picture like this to imply how pleasant life could be if we just buy and drink their products.

though: They want to help us form our opinions, and they want to influence our actions.

Thousands of ads like these bombard people every day. Like all propaganda, these ads are designed to persuade. They aim at their targets carefully, and they create a momentum of social approval that is hard to resist. With all this pressure, how can anyone manage to think for him- or herself?

1

Who Is Running This Show?

*M*ost of us develop a "baloney detector" at an early age. Studies show that by the time most kids are eight years old, they can tell the difference between an advertisement and information.[1] They know an ad is trying to sell something. To do that, an ad or a sales pitch may not tell the whole story. It may try to make something look better than it is.

As they get older, most kids begin to notice more ways advertisers, public relations specialists, and politicians try to influence people. Yet, propagandists are so clever, they often slip a trick by even individuals who think they can always spot baloney, or nonsense. A trick slipped by now and then may not be a serious problem. What difference does it make if I buy Sweet Pepper toothpaste instead of Smitty's toothpaste, even if Smitty's does a better job? Not really much. However, propaganda tricks are often used for more sinister purposes—for example, to cheat someone out of all the money he has saved. The stakes can even be life or death.

In these cases, being able to think for ourselves—and resist influences from baloney peddlers—can hold major importance.

What Is Propaganda?

Sometimes people think of propaganda as "stretching the truth." Most propaganda involves twisting the truth, telling half-truths, or putting a "spin" on the truth. However, one of the most important things to know about propaganda is its purpose.

Let us begin by looking at some common definitions of "propaganda." The *Kingfisher Illustrated Children's Dictionary* says propaganda is "information presented so as to influence public feeling." This same dictionary demonstrates that propaganda has many uses by showing an illustration of giant political campaign posters used at a meeting of the Communist party in Shanghai, China, in 1948. The caption points out that "Propaganda posters are used to great effect for such things as road safety campaigns and health warnings." Propaganda is used for many purposes—large and small. It is not possible to identify propaganda by its subject matter. Also, propaganda may be conveyed by images or even sounds instead of words. Images can be powerful agents of propaganda. For example, the giant posters of political figures suggest power, wisdom, and importance.[2]

Webster's College Dictionary expands the definition. According to this source, propaganda is:

1. information or ideas methodically spread to promote or injure a cause, movement, nation, etc.
2. the deliberate spreading of such information or ideas
3. the particular doctrines or principles propagated by an organization or movement
4. [capitalized] a committee of cardinals, established in 1622 by Pope Gregory XV, having supervision over foreign missions and the training of priests for these missions.[3]

This definition begins to show more about the nature of propaganda. The definition says propaganda is methodical. That is, it is planned and organized to achieve its purpose: to persuade. Also, the spreading of propaganda is deliberate. That is, the person, organization, or business that uses propaganda is acting intentionally and with a purpose. From the point of view of the propagandist, the larger the number of people who see or hear the message, the better.

The dictionary also explains that the word "propaganda" came from a Latin source. It is an abbreviation for the name of a committee formed by the Roman Catholic Church in 1622, the Sacred Congregation for Propagating the Faith. (The Latin version of the committee name is *Sacra Congregatio de Propaganda Fide.*) So, the word "propaganda" is a form of the Latin word that means "to propagate."

To follow the trail a little further, the verb "to propagate" means to spread to a larger number or a wider area. In the case of propaganda, "to propagate" means to spread an idea or opinion to a greater number of people.

The opening paragraph of the article on "propaganda" in the 1997 edition of the *Grolier Multimedia Encyclopedia,* published on CD-ROM, begins with this definition:

Propaganda is the systematic attempt to manipulate the attitudes, beliefs, and actions of people through the use of symbols such as words, gestures, slogans, flags, and uniforms. Ideas, facts, or allegations are spread to further a cause or to damage an opposing cause. The factor that distinguishes propagandizing from educating and informing is deliberate selectivity and manipulation.[4]

The last sentence of this entry raises some interesting questions. It says that propaganda is not the same as educating or informing. What makes the difference? According to the encyclopedia, a propagandist purposefully selects and manipulates what part of the truth or what "facts" (true or not) the audience hears or sees.

Many Motives

Who uses propaganda, and why? The goals of these "persuaders"—people who try to convince or persuade—are not always bad. Sometimes they have wholesome, healthy goals. For example, maybe they are trying to convince expectant mothers not to smoke. Maybe they are campaigning against the illegal use of drugs. Sometimes persuaders have self-centered goals. For example, a saleswoman would like to sell a new computer so she can earn a commission. Sometimes organizations or agencies may design a public-interest billboard or a television advertising spot that is intended to help. An antismoking billboard campaign may advise, "Do not send your future up in smoke."

The tricks of propaganda are available for anyone to use. Propagandists often aim for strong emotional responses to accomplish their goals, and those goals

People even use propaganda in campaigns for good causes. This photo was used in an antismoking campaign to help people realize that smoking while pregnant endangers the life of the unborn child.

are not always honorable. Propaganda's power can be great—unless members of the audience think critically, know their own minds, and pay attention to why they make their decisions. Most important, they need to make sure they are making the decisions they really want and that they are "running their own show."

2

Why Do People Use Propaganda?

*I*n times of war, propaganda can become an important psychological tool to use against the enemy. It is also a powerful method for building morale in one's own nation. It can promote a willingness to make sacrifices and to support the nation's cause.

After terrorists attacked the World Trade Center and the Pentagon on September 11, 2001, morale-building slogans could be seen everywhere. Businesses, health clinics, Web sites, government offices, and people's homes displayed signs bearing slogans such as "UNITED WE STAND," "FREEDOM IS NOT FREE," and "GOD BLESS AMERICA." These emotional phrases touched a chord of hope and determination in many people. The intention was to encourage people to feel that America was in the right and that they should be willing to make sacrifices to defend their nation.

Many people used just a symbol—the American flag—to convey all these ideas. They flew the flag from their cars and in front of their homes, and they placed it in the windows of businesses and offices.

Whether or not one agrees with all these ideas, the objectives of the slogans are easy to see. Many Americans had lost friends and family members in the attacks. Most Americans felt frightened and anxious. These slogans helped rebuild a sense of pride and purpose. Because the attackers had used commercial airliners as flying suicide bombs, flying now seemed more risky than before. What would the terrorists do next? Would they succeed in hijacking other planes? The federal government set up new standards for making sure airliners would be safe. Baggage checks were more thorough. People were searched. Flying was not as free and easy as before. Slogans encouraged people who had lost some freedoms to see their loss as necessary and even desirable. The slogans encouraged people to feel that complaining was "anti-American."

Not everyone thought that this emotional response was entirely positive, though. Some people voiced the opinion that important and even dangerous losses of freedom had begun to make inroads on Constitutional rights. In the words of newspaperwoman Janis Besler Heaphy, "No one argues the validity and need for both retaliation and security. But to what lengths are we willing to go to achieve them? Specifically, to what degree are we willing to compromise our civil liberties in the name of security?" In particular, she expressed concern about freedom of the press and the public's right to know. She cited several occasions in the months following September 11 when the federal administration had pressured news organizations, such as television news programs and newspapers, to withhold information from their listeners and readers.

Many people think strong arguments exist in support of the government's actions. Citizens are justifiably anxious and feel a need to know what decisions are being made and what is going on. However, whatever they know will also be information that terrorists will have and use. In these circumstances, the nation's safety and security may well require that some facts be kept secret.

Nonetheless, Heaphy was raising important points. The government is controlling information and that really is a form of propaganda. Is that fair? Do the rules change when a nation's liberty is at stake? What if lives are at risk? Many people think that a government has no choice, knowing that the enemy can use propaganda, too—and usually will. Not everyone thinks so, though. Heaphy quotes Thomas Friedman of *The New York Times*, who asserted: "We have to fight terrorists as if there are no rules . . . and preserve our open society as if there were no terrorists."[1]

A Long Tradition

Propaganda first became an important war-time weapon during World War I—the "Great War." The war began in 1914. By then, Europe had divided into two groups: the Central Powers (Germany, Austria-Hungary, Bulgaria, and Turkey) and the Allied Powers (Great Britain, the British Empire, France, Belgium, Russia, and Italy). The United States also became one of the Allied Powers in 1917.

Just before joining the Allies, the United States founded a group called the U.S. Committee on Public Information (CPI). Its job was to promote the war to Americans. Many Americans did not want their country involved in the war. They did not want to send young

American men into a battle they felt was Europe's battle, not theirs. The CPI's message to Americans was: The United States should be involved in the war. It was a good cause. The enemy was evil. American soldiers were heroic. If they would join their friends in Europe in this fight, this would be "the war to end all wars."[2]

The CPI had volunteers in towns all across America. These were men who promoted the war in their home-towns. When a newspaper criticized the United States for entering the war, the volunteers had "canned" speeches that they made at meetings. That is, they used ready-made addresses over and over—no matter where they were from or where they spoke. They encouraged and urged and stirred up patriotism. These were "grassroots" propagandists. They were people known in their community, part of "the guys"—not outsiders from the state capital or from Washington, D.C.

When the United States entered World War II in 1941, the propagandists went to work again. With most of the nation's men called into the armed forces, who was going to run the factories? The government began a campaign to encourage women to go to work in the place of the men. "Rosie the Riveter" became a national poster queen. She knew how to weld rivets and build airplanes. She worked with steel. She was strong, yet feminine. Her message rang out from the posters: "We Can Do It!" It was one of the most successful promotions of the time. Thousands of women went to work and gained experience they had never had before. They found they could do it. So, a campaign intended to aid the waging of war turned out to have more than one outcome. Not only did these women keep the country going, they also gained new confidence and new skills.

When the war was over, the economy entered a boom

With America's young men nearly all in the armed services, women began to take jobs in factories for the first time. A powerful "We Can Do It!" ad campaign showed "Rosie the Riveter" looking glamorous, capable, and proud to serve her country.

period. Men came back to their old jobs, but many women did not stop working. Many continued in the factories and offices—often paid less than their male counterparts. However, from that time on, women have formed a major part of the American workforce. Today, women are still not always treated equally in the workplace. However, women now fly fighter jets, perform surgery, become corporate leaders, and enter many professions that used to be considered "for men only." Some of these developments can be said to have begun when "Rosie the Riveter" and her coworkers broke the social patterns of their time—encouraged, strangely enough, by propaganda.

Using Fear and Shame

In Britain during World War I, propagandists urged women to encourage the men in their lives to sign up for military service. These propagandists certainly believed that their motives were good. They felt an urgency. Britain needed to protect itself, and the country needed men. The important thing to look at is the way persuasive techniques were used, though. An example of a poster from that time is on the next page.

This poster played on the women's emotions. The first two points play on fear: Look what has happened to other countries. Your home, too, can be destroyed. You and your neighbors could be killed.

The third point calls the audience to action: You can make a difference. It also calls for a sense of responsibility and patriotism: Do this for your king and country.

The fourth point evokes shame: Will your loved one be among those who did not help when your country needed him? It also settles responsibility on its audience: "because you would not let him go."

TO THE WOMEN OF BRITAIN

1. You have read what the Germans have done in Belgium. Have you thought what they would do if they invaded this Country?

2. Do you realise that the safety of your home and children depends on our getting more men NOW?

3. Do you realise that the one word "GO" from you may send another man to fight for our King and Country?

4. When the War is over and someone asks your husband or your son what he did in the Great War, is he to hang his head because you would not let him go?

WON'T YOU HELP AND SEND A MAN TO JOIN THE ARMY TO-DAY?

Propagandists also dropped leaflets over enemy territory. For example, French propagandists printed up a leaflet made to look as if it came from German soldiers in French prison camps. "Pass this along," the leaflet invited. "German War Comrades!" it continued, "Think about this:

"1. Only greedy rulers want war. The people want peace, and work, and bread.

"2. Only the German Kaiser (leader) with his militarists, Junkers, and arms manufacturers wanted war, prepared for it and brought it on. . . .

"10. Stop fighting! Turn your cannons around! Come over to us. Shoot anyone who wants to hinder you from coming."[3]

With leaflets like this one, the Allied propagandists hoped to discourage enemy troops and citizens. They tried to undermine their morale. Their words attacked Germany's military leaders. They encouraged soldiers to defect and even to shoot fellow soldiers who tried to stop them.

Propaganda has often been used to stir up hatred and fear within countries as well. The following two examples of hate propaganda used within a country had disastrous results: hate killing in Rwanda and the Holocaust in Germany.

Rwanda: Terror by Radio

Rwanda is a small country located in central Africa. Its population is composed of two main groups of people, the Tutsi and the Hutu. Throughout most of Rwanda's history, these two groups lived quite peacefully side by side. In 1916, however, Belgian colonists arrived and took over the running of the country. They supported a Tutsi monarchy for most of that time. Then bloody Hutu rebellions broke out after the death of the Tutsi king in 1959. Many Tutsi were killed. So, the Belgian colonial leaders shifted their support to a Hutu government, hoping this move would calm the country down. The Hutu government declared Rwanda an independent republic in 1961, but the battles were not over.

When the colonists withdrew, they left behind an ugly new tradition—deep distrust between Tutsi and Hutu. Many bloody conflicts took place. Then the president of Rwanda, a Hutu, was assassinated in 1994. Many Rwandans blamed the assassination on Tutsi rebels.

Hutu leaders began a heavy radio propaganda campaign. They set up their own radio station, the "Mille Collines" (a thousand hills). The name identified the radio station with the listeners' country, a land with thousands of hills. The radio station played popular music. Between songs, however, announcers told their listeners to "kill the Tutsi cockroaches." They read lists of Tutsi names, pointing them out for execution.

Hutu listeners were already afraid. Their president had been killed. The anti-Tutsi radio broadcasts told the Hutu that the Tutsi would take their lives if they did not act first. Even though many Tutsi were their neighbors and long-time friends, the radio station's messages were convincing. Week after week, the named Tutsi were found dead, often hunted down in their homes or in the streets. Many were stabbed with machetes and knives handed out by militia (citizens organized for military action). Between April and June of 1994, nearly 1 million Tutsi and moderate Hutu citizens were killed.[4] Nearly 2 million Hutu also fled from their homes and country—chased out by avenging Tutsi. The Rwandan massacres are considered among the worst of the twentieth century. The powerful propaganda campaign of Mille Collines took a heavy and terrible human toll.

Against the Jews: Calculated Hatred

Adolf Hitler rose to power in Germany in 1933. One of his first decisions was to appoint a minister, or chief, of propaganda. He chose a man named Paul Joseph Goebbels, an intelligent, well-educated man. Hitler put Goebbels in charge of popular enlightenment and propaganda.

Goebbels had full control of all information sources and media: newspapers, radio, movies, theater, books, poetry, and art. He blocked out information he did not want the German people to know about. Goebbels also developed a huge campaign that promoted Hitler's government and the Nazi party. Germany was the greatest nation in the world, his campaigners trumpeted. They declared that the German people were the best in the world. If Germany had troubles and shortcomings, they said, one group of people was to blame: the Jews. During the following decade, German officials convinced many German citizens that Jewish members of their community should be imprisoned and killed—just because they were Jewish.

More than 6 million Jews were killed by the Nazi government in Germany between 1933 and 1945. Friends and neighbors stood by while police took away Jewish families at gunpoint. The families were loaded onto boxcars and shipped to concentration camps, where they were sometimes used as slave labor until they died of starvation or disease. Others were executed in gas chambers.

Why did people stand by and let innocent people be imprisoned and killed? One of the biggest reasons was that they thought they were doing the right thing. They had been convinced by the propaganda put out by Goebbels and his hate campaign.

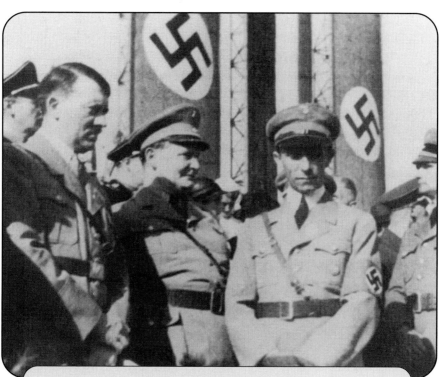

Adolf Hitler and his minister of propaganda, Joseph Goebbels, knew how to stir large crowds to a frenzied approval of even the most excessive Nazi programs.

How Did It Happen?

It is easy to see how dangerous propaganda was in these examples. Think about what it would be like to be a Tutsi in Rwanda or a Jew in Germany during each of these times. Children and old people, mothers and fathers, aunts and uncles, brothers and sisters all were killed. Why did people listen to leaders who asked them to kill their neighbors? Why did they let their friends be dragged away and killed? Because they believed the propaganda. They were persuaded that these acts were their own best protection. They became convinced that following such instructions was the right thing to do.

Thinking for Oneself

The examples in this chapter show what a serious problem propaganda can be. Yet, in a mild form, propaganda is all around us, every day. Marketing and advertising executives make use of persuasion to sell products. They use it to build positive images for businesses. Politicians try to gain votes on election day by smiling, agreeing with everyone, and cooing at babies. Who would not vote for someone who liked babies? Even charities use sales techniques to convince people to give money to their cause. Occasionally, so do teachers and parents—and kids. For example, a child tries to persuade his parents by pleading, "Aw, please, all the kids are doing it!" Anyone who wants to persuade other people of a point of view, attitude, or belief will very likely use some of these techniques at one time or another.

The trouble is that someone with bad intentions can be just as persuasive as someone with good intentions. So it is a healthy practice to have a well-developed "propaganda radar." Recognize the techniques. Calm down the emotional reactions usually raised by persuasive methods. Then calmly think about the real message and think about whether it seems reasonable. The following two chapters discuss some of the tools and tricks persuaders use. Understanding these techniques makes them easier to resist.

3

How Persuaders Use Emotion

What makes humans tick? What is the best way to influence someone? Playing on human emotions can be a very effective approach. Fear, hate, loneliness, the need for friendship and love, insecurity, patriotism, love for one's mother, pride, the desire to look cool—the list of powerful emotions goes on and on. Images, symbols, and music that speak to those emotions are some of the persuader's favorite tools.

Using Images

As the saying goes, "A picture is worth a thousand words." Look at any campaign poster photo. It gives the voter a face to vote for. The smile makes the candidate look like a friend. This is someone, the voter thinks, who will do some good for our school, our city, or our state. This is someone who will do some good for me.

Propagandists use pictures to identify their causes with positive or negative emotions. A politician's publicist distributes photos of the candidate holding a baby. What is the spin—the interpretation observers are supposed to make? People may find themselves assuming that the candidate respects motherhood and family. This candidate, they may conclude, will support programs for helping today's youth—for example, day care, schools, and training programs. These assumptions may be formed consciously or subconsciously.

By combining an effective picture with a strong slogan, a poster, a billboard, or a television spot can make a powerful, persuasive statement. Recently, as part of its "Don't Buy the Lie" antitobacco program, a health management organization (HMO) cosponsored a poster contest for middle-school students in the Greater Sacramento region in California. The winner was Chris Gates, an eighth grader at Andrew Carnegie Middle School. His design called for a giant photo of an ashtray full of cigarette butts, displayed with his slogan: "Ashes, ashes, we all fall down." This poster was displayed on billboards viewed by more than 750,000 people and was a powerful piece of propaganda— this time, propaganda for health. The poster displayed an unpleasant image that even cigarette smokers usually dislike. Its slogan was part of a familiar childhood jingle. The innocence of the jingle contrasted with the distasteful photo caught people's attention. The poster also gave a new meaning to the jingle by reminding viewers that cigarette smoking can cause their downfall. By combining graphics with a short, clever slogan, this eighth grader made a strong, persuasive statement for the antitobacco cause.[1]

A British artist drew this frightening cartoon during World War I to stir up hatred against the man shown in the center of the drawing, William II, emperor of Germany. Notice the use of symbols: a skull as a symbol for death; a snake as "evil" German culture ("Kultur"); the devil; a vulture; a hangman's noose; poison. The torn document on the table stands for broken agreements between Germany and its neighbors.

Symbols of Hate and Love

Symbols are simple shapes that can represent complicated ideas, concepts, and emotions. Flash a symbol and most people experience an instant reaction. A flag can be a powerful symbol for a nation's people. The Nazi swastika began as a symbol of power and national pride. However, because most people associate it with the Holocaust and hatred of Jews, it has become a symbol of hate. The Christian cross has become a symbol of all Christian religions. For Christians today, it may be a comforting reminder. It may help them recall a religious motto, such as "Love your neighbor." During the Crusades in the Middle Ages, though, Christian armies marched on Jerusalem. Then, the cross became a symbol of war, worn on shields and clothing.

Propagandists like to use symbols because they are both simple and powerful. By using the swastika, the Nazi party in Germany could instantly remind people of their national pride. The symbol stood for strong bodies, intelligence, success, and the world leadership Hitler told them they deserved. Party leaders knew the positive feelings of pride and self-worth that the German people attached to the swastika symbol. The Nazi party used the swastika's positive appeal to gain acceptance for all Nazi policies— including the Holocaust, the result of a set of policies that included the persecution and execution of 6 million Jews and 4 million blacks, homosexuals, and disabled persons. Today the swastika has become a symbol of hate. People worldwide identify the swastika with the Holocaust and the belief systems that fed it.

The Magic of Music

Music is a universal language. Babies respond to its rhythms before they learn to understand or speak words.

Music cuts across cultures and can communicate directly with human emotions. Listen sometime to the score playing in the background during a tense scene in a movie. Notice how it helps create an edgy and nervous atmosphere. In the United States, a march by John Philip Sousa can make hearts pound with patriotic pride. The drumbeats echo the heartbeat of life, and the patterns of the rhythm produce natural responses. A rapper's rhythm works with the words to produce emotions—maybe anger, exhilaration, or a sense of justice. Music forms a basic part of every culture. It creates a bond among people. It makes people—even tiny toddlers—want to dance to its rhythms. There is nothing wrong with all this. It is part of the beauty of being human.

A propagandist, though, can use music to stir up emotions at a rally. An advertiser may use music to convey a message in a television commercial. Many people do not consciously notice the music. It is just part of the package. However, our emotions respond to the whole presentation—the words, the images, the symbols, and the music. The overall effect can sweep the observer along in a swell of emotion that persuades. Most important, the effect may influence decisions and actions.

4

Watching for Twists in Language and Logic

The important point to remember about propaganda is to be aware of the techniques. Watch for the sales pitch and understand how it works. Once the persuasive edge is recognized, it is disarmed. It no longer has the same power, and it is easier to make objective decisions and avoid being manipulated unfairly. It is important to be able to tell the difference between straight information or educational material and a clear attempt to persuade.

The use of persuasive terms and approaches does not automatically make anyone a "bad guy." However, persuasive techniques do make use of tricks. Sometimes they are like a magician's sleight of hand—now you see it, and now you don't. It is important first to know who is talking and what that person is trying to accomplish. Second, it is vital to recognize what techniques are being used.

Who Is Talking and Why?

Does the writer or speaker have a special agenda, or list of goals to accomplish? Sometimes this agenda is disguised (a "hidden agenda"). Then it is necessary to dig for it—play detective. Look for motives. Are there special reasons for telling a particular story? What are the reasons? Do the facts make a special point? What is the writer's or speaker's objective?

Often, the speaker wants to make money. A friend hopes to sell an old skateboard. He says it is the best skateboard he has ever had. If so, though, why does he want to sell it? Maybe he explains that he wants a new one. It may be the best he has ever had, but it is not the best he ever hopes to have. Is it worth the money he is asking? Is it good enough? Or will the new buyer want a new one, too, before very long? Then, the money may already be spent on a skateboard that really was not good enough in the first place.

Money is not the only possible motive. Sometimes the persuader wants power. Politicians want the power they gain by winning an election, so they make promises and speeches to get people to vote for them. They often use all the techniques of propaganda to persuade people to vote for them. Are they being honest, or are they misrepresenting themselves? If their listeners peel away the propaganda techniques, what is left? Does the candidate have an honest program that will benefit the voters?

The Language of Propaganda

Here are a few ways propagandists use language.[1]

- **Bandwagon**—This is persuading people by telling them that "other people are doing it."

In this satirical cartoon, the cartoonist seems to be pointing out how much people are influenced by their own way of looking at things. From the perspective of the Communist flag at the top left, the worker on the roof is "bigger than life"—he is much larger compared to the buildings than a normal man would be. However, what the artist at the bottom "sees"—and paints—is a murdering pirate.

Humans are social. They like to be part of the group. Knowing that other people believe something or have agreed to something makes it sound like a good thing to believe or do. In school, someone might say, "All the kids are doing it." An ad for a diet aid might claim, "More dieters use 'KwikLoss' than any other brand."

However, the decision is really up to you. It is a good idea to get more information before jumping onto any bandwagon. Why are so many kids carrying backpacks or smoking or wearing $98 sports shoes? Try finding out what their reasons are. Why are so many people using KwikLoss? Is it cheaper? Does it do a better job? Does it taste better? Do medical professionals recommend it? Or maybe it just has cuter commercials. It probably would be a good idea to know more about the product before using it.

- **Appeal to authority**—This involves using a figure of authority or a famous person to recommend or endorse a belief or activity. Just like the bandwagon approach, this is another form of value by association. For example, an Olympic gold medal swimmer's picture appears on a package of "Breakfast Yummies" cereal. The implied message: "You, too, can be an Olympic star . . . if you start your day with Breakfast Yummies!" Or, at least, the consumer is encouraged to think that a breakfast cereal that is good enough for a gold medalist must be good for them, too.

- **Misleading with numbers**—This is the use of a statistic or percentage to impress (even though the numbers may not really be impressive). An advertisement may claim that 10 percent of doctors recommend MagnaMagnets for curing broken toenails. Ten percent is not a high percentage, however, so why should anyone be impressed? Also, what study showed this statistic? How many doctors were surveyed? Exactly what question did the survey pose? What does the ad mean by "doctor?" This, by the way, is also an appeal to authority. Notice how the propagandist has piled one persuasive technique on top of another, for a double hit.

- **Glittering generalities**—This entails making broad, general statements that could fit anything or anyone and so have no significant meaning. Phrases such as "the best that money can buy" can mean something different to everyone. The expression "Let's make America strong again" can mean "Let's build up our military might," or "Let's build a strong economy." It might suggest "Let's work together instead of fighting each other." The phrase could have many other meanings, as well. A phrase like, "Let's destroy evil wherever we find it" can have many meanings, depending on who is listening.

What do "best," "strong," and "evil" mean in these examples? These are glittering generalities—expressions that may sound good, but can leave different people with different impressions. As a result, people could find themselves agreeing with a certain statement without recognizing or understanding the speaker's full intended meaning.

- **Repetition**—This is saying a motto, slogan, or brand name over and over until it sticks in people's minds as right, true, or just plain memorable. Many advertisers use a rule of thumb: Repeat the product name at least four times in a commercial. They are hoping that the more the customers hear the brand name, the more likely they will buy the product. In the same way, repetition of an idea may lead people to feel they agree—the words become familiar and perhaps therefore they may seem "right."

- **Emotional words**—By using words that stir up emotion, writers and speakers can sway even the most careful thinker. They may use any of a wide range of emotions, such as fear, sentimentality, patriotism, sense of family, loyalty, and pride. Fear can be especially persuasive.

Logical Fallacies

A *fallacy* is an untrue statement or argument based on false or invalid reasoning. Experts have identified nearly fifty common fallacies that may creep into arguments and persuasive discussions. Sometimes writers and speakers rely on these fallacies innocently, without realizing what they are doing. Often, though, they do use false reasoning on purpose, hoping to fool readers and listeners into looking at a topic a certain way. In either case, truth and accuracy get lost in the shuffle. Here are just a few of the most common of these blocks to clear thinking and honest discussion.[2]

- **Appeal to emotion**—This is used in place of logical reasoning, since an argument is not made true just because one is fearful, proud, or loves one's country. This trick is so powerful that it deserves a place among the prime examples of unclear thinking known as fallacies.

- **Personal attack** (also known by its Latin name, *Ad hominem*)—This method attacks the person putting forth an idea. For example, "Look at the candidate's stupid yellow tie. Would you want a class president who wears such dorky clothes?" This fashion critique might have a place at a fashion show, but what does it have to do with a candidate's qualifications for office?

  People often try to "prove" that their opponents are wrong or lying by attacking them personally. For example, Jon says to Michael, "You took my pen." Michael defends himself, "No I did not." Jon retorts, "Everyone knows you are a born liar." Does that prove the point? What evidence can Jon show for any of his claims? And even if Michael does have a reputation for lying, that does not prove that he is lying now or that he took Jon's pen.

- **Flattery**—This can be a good way to distract a listener's attention from the soundness of an argument. An ad might begin like this: "You dig great music. You know cool when you hear it. So, we are sure you will appreciate the new CD just out from Les Belles Dames. . . ."

- **Begging the question**—This means drawing a conclusion based on a premise that still needs to be established or proven. The premise may actually be true, but the speaker or writer has not proved it. An example might be, "Prisons are necessary because without them the crime rate would skyrocket." (Would it? Maybe so—but the writer should provide some evidence.)

    As another example, assume that Tim is supposed to debate the question, "Would a student council be good for this school?" But instead of presenting his argument proving that it *would* be helpful, Tim starts off by launching his election campaign: "You should vote for me for student council because I understand what students want!" This assumes that the original question has already been settled.

    Begging the question could involve circular reasoning, which essentially restates the premise without proving it: "You should not steal, because you should not take someone else's things." Since "steal" means "to take someone else's things" by definition, the two parts of the sentence say the same thing, without ever really explaining *why* you should not steal.

- **Red herring**—This technique distracts attention with a completely unrelated comment. Red herrings often carry some emotional baggage to draw the reader in. For example, a television campaign spot for a political candidate might mention that her husband is a successful stockbroker. Listeners who admire wealth and success may tend to transfer that approval to his wife, even though she is running for office, not her husband.

- **Straw man**—This approach makes the speaker's position appear strong by portraying the opposition as weaker than it really is (setting up an opposition made of straw and then knocking it down). For example, an ad might state: "Senator Jones thinks we should spend less on health care for the elderly. Apparently she thinks that people over 65 have plenty of extra money lying around." In reality, she probably does not think that at all. What does she think? Obviously this source has no interest in providing the answer.

- **Card stacking**—This involves leaving out important facts or using just a portion of the evidence to make an argument appear stronger. For example, a salesperson may tell only the strong points of a computer game that is for sale, but he may fail to mention that without a huge hard disk, it runs too slowly to be any fun to play.

Many of these fallacies are like a magician's tricks. They use sleight of hand to distract the listener's or reader's attention and then draw an unwarranted conclusion. Or they substitute something that appears to be the real thing but is not—something counterfeit. The art of catching fallacies can be practiced by reading any magazine, newspaper, book, or Web site. Faulty reasoning is all around. Take a look and prepare to be surprised at how common it is.

Looking at an Argument

The courtroom is one place where clear thinking about arguments or statements people make is especially important. Jury members face the same challenges other people face every day, but under more pressure. They must listen carefully as attorneys plead the case at hand. They need to understand what special tricks or deceptions the attorneys may be using to persuade. The jury's task is especially urgent, since their decision may affect the lives of many people. For example, the life of the defendant, or accused, may be at stake. Other people involved in the case may be affected.

For jury members—and for regular people in everyday life—two key points are the most important to consider, according to Bruce Waller, author of *Critical Thinking: Consider the Verdict*. He asks, "Is the argument *valid*, and are the *premises* of the argument actually *true*?" That is, first: Does the conclusion follow logically from the premise or premises? Second: Are the premises true statements? An argument is not sound unless the answers to both these questions are "Yes." In other words, what is the speaker trying to prove, and did he or she prove it? The persuader's tricks and techniques are good to know, but these two basic questions can help cut through a lot of extra fluff and get straight to the core of each statement.[3]

A premise is a statement or group of statements from which one draws a conclusion. When someone tries to convince or persuade, he or she usually uses a set of statements that together form an argument. For example:

1. Joe hit a home run every time he was at bat this spring.

2. At Joe's school, hitters who hit the ball every time they are at bat always receive a special trophy.

3. Joe will receive a trophy.

In this example, the first two statements are premises. Their purpose is to lay the groundwork of the argument by stating basic facts. The third statement is the conclusion. The conclusion should follow logically from the stated premises.

However, what if one or both of the first statements is false? Here is an example:

1. If the moon is made of green cheese, then there are mice on the moon.

2. The moon is made of green cheese.

3. Therefore, there are mice on the moon.

This example is a little silly, but it shows an important point. Everyone knows there are no mice on the moon. Yet this conclusion is logical, given the premises.

So what is wrong with this example? The premises are false. Everyone knows the moon is not made of green cheese. This example shows that no matter how good the logic is, if an argument starts out with a false premise—that is, if an argument is based on an untrue statement—it will lead to a false conclusion.

Consider this conversation as it might take place among a group of friends:

Person A: Want some (drug)?
Person B: No.
Person A: What are you, chicken?
Person B: No.
Person A: Well, then, try some!

Broken down as parts of an argument, the same conversation looks like this:

1. If you do not try the drug, you are chicken (scared).
2. You are not chicken.
3. Therefore you will (should) try the drug.

This argument is very dangerous, but because of the way it is stated, it seems logical. What is wrong with the argument? First of all, it is based on the false premise that if you do not want to smoke, it must be because you are scared. Since that premise is false—there could be any number of reasons why a person would not want to smoke—it leads to a false conclusion.

In addition to starting with a false premise, this argument piles on a *second* fallacy in the conclusion—that if a certain statement is true, then its reverse must also be true. Statement 1 says that if you do not want to smoke, you are scared. But Statements 2 and 3 assume the reverse: that if you are not scared, then you will want to smoke. Even if Statement 1 were true, that would not automatically mean the reverse was true.

The argument also uses another unfair tool. Person A is

trying to manipulate, or "get at," Person B by using Person B's fear that other people might think he or she is scared.

Anyone might be trapped by an argument like this one, but that does not have to happen. The next chapter explores ways to overcome such an argument by revealing the flaws and not being fooled by them.

5

Ducking the Noose

*P*ropagandists swing a noose above our heads to catch us and reel us in. They want to convince or persuade. They want to sell people on their ideas or products. Propagandists want people to do or think what they think people should do or think. No one really wants to be a victim. No one really wants to be fooled, or reeled in. Most people want to think for themselves. Yet, with so many persuaders trying to convince them to buy, vote, use their influence, and think in particular ways, how can anyone duck all the traps?

Be Prepared

Expect efforts to persuade. Studies have shown that knowing about the tricks and methods of persuasion is not

When a person is always in the middle of things, acting and reacting, it can be difficult to see patterns or question other people's motives. One way to keep from being taken in by propaganda is to do a lot of reading, observing, and thinking on one's own.

a "vaccination" against becoming persuaded. Teens who have learned about bandwagons and glittering generalities still tend to buy advertised brands. Most adults buy the most heavily advertised brands—just because they are advertised.[1]

One study, though, showed that advance warning helped. A group of teens were told that they would hear a presentation on "Why Teenagers Should Not Be Allowed to Drive." When the speaker began ten minutes later, this group was prepared, and few of them were convinced by the arguments. A second group, though, received no warning. The speaker just began presenting the arguments against teenage driving. This group was taken by surprise, and most of them were convinced the arguments were valid.[2]

Unfortunately, no one can count on being warned. So, it is a good idea to be aware when a sales pitch is likely. Imagine a customer walking into a store, and the salesperson suddenly appears. "Welcome to Shady Deals, Inc.," she says with a smile. "We're having a special two-for-one sale today on name-brand YousslussUglée capris."

Probably buying even one pair of YousslussUglée capris was not really the customer's reason for going to the store that day. But whenever a customer walks into a store, someone is likely to try to make a sale. That is how salespeople earn money. So remember the old adage, "A fool and his (or her) money are soon parted." Put another way, buying or otherwise acting on impulse or under pressure may be a mistake.

This buyer, though, is expecting a sales pitch. So, she is not so easily steered toward capri pants she does not really want to buy.

Of course, maybe the shopper really likes YousslussUglée capris. The colors are great and the two-for-one offer looks like a good deal. In that case, the shopper is listening to her own priorities—not the salesperson's. The shopper is thinking for herself.

Dress Rehearsal

Another good method for dealing with propaganda is to practice a strong response to an expected argument. For example, suppose a teacher asks a group for their opinions about a proposed statewide ninth-grade examination. Each member of the group expresses an opinion, but then that opinion is mildly attacked. The students defend their opinions. By practicing responses to mild objection, the students are better prepared to handle opposition. Then later, when the school principal expresses very strong disagreement with the students' opinions, those students who have already practiced defending their point of view are less easily persuaded.[3]

So, in the example of the persistent salesperson, the shopper may smile politely, and perhaps she even thanks the salesperson for the tip. Then she may say, "I would like to look around and see what else you have, while I am here." Usually a salesperson recognizes this as a subtle request to back off. She may offer her name or say she will be nearby if there are any questions. She may take a last stab at the two-for-one capri sale by indicating their location. However, the customer's simple prepared comment helped sidestep the salesperson's persuasive approach. Without a salesperson hovering close by, a customer can often make clearer comparisons and less hassled decisions about what she or he may really want to buy. If the side stepping has been done pleasantly, the salesperson's help will still be available when it is needed.

In one study, researchers took a look at what would happen when a group of seventh graders received instruction

Practicing a reply and role playing can help overcome the impact of propaganda.

about what to do when confronted with the pressure to smoke a cigarette. They viewed a series of advertisements for cigarettes that congratulated women for gaining the freedom to smoke. Then instructors presented the idea that women who were truly liberated would not give up their freedom by allowing themselves to be hooked on tobacco. Also they did some role playing. A group would play the role of friends trying to get a teen to smoke, calling him a coward if he refused. Each member of the group had a chance to practice a retort, such as "I would be a real coward if I smoked just to impress you," or "I think it takes more courage *not* to smoke."

This kind of practice worked for these teens. The study showed that even two years later, when this group of teens reached ninth grade, fewer of them smoked than in another group that attended a similar junior high but had not been through a similar role-playing program.

Practicing a good response to a powerful argument is one of the strongest defenses against propaganda and persuasion.[4]

Playing "Devil's Advocate"

Sometimes, a situation comes up without warning and with no chance to practice a response. This requires thinking on one's feet. A good method is to play "devil's advocate." That is, think of the situation from the other person's point of view—argue for the other person's agenda, to yourself. Good chess players learn to do this well. What is the other guy up to? What is the opponent's strategy? Why did she make that move? What does she have to gain? What do I have to lose?

Asking these kinds of questions presents a new, fresh view of what is going on. In the case of handling a

Good chess players practice seeing things from the other player's view. Looking at things from the other person's perspective is a useful skill in life, as well. It can help in understanding the other side's motives and objectives—and can even help a person recognize and respond to propaganda.

persuader, think about why choices are presented in a certain way. What other choices are available that the persuader has not mentioned? What does that tell about the persuader and the persuader's goals? What consequences would a different choice bring?

Remember, all propaganda is an attempt to sell something—usually a product, a service, or an idea. Sometimes the product, service, or idea being sold may be desirable, useful, or beneficial. Sometimes it is not. Propaganda can be used for good or for bad. The trick is to understand how it works and when it is being used. As another famous saying goes, "Doubt is the beginning of wisdom."[5] So, keep that "baloney detector" well-tuned!

Chapter Notes

Chapter 1. Who Is Running This Show?

1. Anthony R. Pratkanis and Elliot Aronson, *The Age of Propaganda: The Everyday Use and Abuse of Persuasion* (New York: W. H. Freeman & Company, 1992), p. 208.

2. *Kingfisher Illustrated Children's Dictionary*, First American Edition (New York: Kingfisher, 1994), p. 325.

3. *Random House Webster's College Dictionary* (New York: Random House, 2000), p. 1061.

4. *Grolier Multimedia Encyclopedia*, Deluxe Edition CD-ROM (New York: Grolier Interactive Inc., 1997).

Chapter 2. Why Do People Use Propaganda?

1. Janis Besler Heaphy, publisher and president of the *Sacramento Bee*, in a mid-year commencement address published by the *Sacramento Bee*, Sacramento, California, December 17, 2001 <http://www.sacbee.com/content/news/projects/attacks/story/13399654p-1409462c.html> (February 13, 2002).

2. Stuart Ewen, *PR! A Social History of Spin* (New York: Basic Books, 1996), p. 104ff.

3. Jane Plotke and Richard Hacken, eds., *Propaganda Leaflets*, February 2, 1996, Harold B. Yee Library, Brigham Young University, n.d. <http://www.lib.byu.edu/~rdh/wwi/1915/propleaf.html> (March 25, 2002).

4. *1999 Grolier Interactive Encyclopedia.* (New York: Grolier Interactive Inc., 1998). National Security Archive Web page, n.d. <http://www.gwu.edu/~nsarchiv/NSAEBB/NSAEBB53/index2.html> (March 25, 2002).

Chapter 3. How Persuaders Use Emotion

1. Blair Anthony Robertson, "Getting Their Message Across," *The Sacramento Bee*, March 8, 2002, p. B3.

Chapter 4. Watching for Twists in Language and Logic

1. Jerry Cederblom and David W. Paulsen, *Critical Reasoning: Understanding and Criticizing Arguments and Theories* (Belmont, Calif.: Wadsworth Publishing Co., 1982), pp. 84–86. Michael C. Labossiere, "Fallacies," 1995 <http://www.nizkor.org/features/fallacies/> (March 25, 2002).

2. Cederblom and Paulsen, pp. 85–86.

3. Bruce N. Waller, *Critical Thinking: Consider the Verdict* (Englewood Cliffs, N.J.: Prentice-Hall, 1988), p. 14.

Chapter 5. Ducking the Noose

1. Anthony R. Pratkanis and Elliot Aronson, *The Age of Propaganda: The Everyday Use and Abuse of Persuasion* (New York: W. H. Freeman & Company, 1992), pp. 208–209.

2. Jonathan L. Freedman and David O. Sears, "Warning, Distraction, and Resistance to Influence," *Journal of Personality and Social Psychology*, 1965, vol. 1 #3, pp. 262–266, as discussed by Pratkanis and Aronson, p. 209.

3. Pratkanis and Aronson, p. 213.

4. Ibid.

5. Often attributed to Clarence Darrow, a criminal defense lawyer who was famous for cutting through tangled facts with tough and critical questions, n.d. <http://www.tatanka.com/reading/humanity/quotes1.htm> (June 11, 2002).

Glossary

advertising—A notice in print or other media (such as television, radio, or billboards) intended to sell or attract attention to a product, service, event, etc.

fallacy—A statement or argument based on false or invalid reasoning.

hate—To act upon or to advocate hostility or violence toward, lies about, or separation from a person or a group of people.

premise—A statement from which a conclusion is drawn.

propaganda—A systematic attempt to influence people through words, pictures, symbols, sounds, uniforms, and so on; propaganda can range from open attempts to persuade to less obvious methods, sometimes using unrelated means to influence a person's opinions or behavior.

spin—To present in a way that is intended to influence how people perceive a fact or event; to apply a special point of view or interpretation.

Further Reading

Barker, Dan, and Brian Strasbourg (illustrator). *Maybe Yes, Maybe No: A Guide for Young Skeptics*. Amherst, N.Y.: Prometheus Books, 1990.

Day, Nancy. *Advertising: Information or Manipulation?* Springfield, N.J.: Enslow Publishers, Inc., 1999.

Pratkanis, Anthony R., and Elliot Aronson. *Age of Propaganda: The Everyday Use and Abuse of Persuasion*, revised edition. New York: W. H. Freeman & Co., 2001.

Roberts, Jeremy. *Joseph Goebbels: Nazi Propaganda Minister*. New York: Rosen Publishing Group, 2000.

Ruchlis, Hy, with Sandra Oddo. *Clear Thinking: A Practical Introduction*. Foreword by Isaac Asimov. New York: Prometheus Books, 1990.

Internet Addresses

Media Awareness (Canada)
Challenging Online Hate
   <http://www.media-awareness.ca/eng/issues/internet/
   hintro.htm>

July 1942: United We Stand
Smithsonian National Museum History
   <http://americanhistory.si.edu/1942/introduction.
   html>

Index